*British*AMERICANS

SPIRIT
of America®

*British*AMERICANS

By Vicky Franchino

Content Adviser: Eliga H. Gould, Associate Professor of History, University of New Hampshire, Durham, North Carolina

The Child's World®
Chanhassen, Minnesota

8

*British*AMERICANS

Published in the United States of America by The Child's World®
P.O. Box 326 • Chanhassen, MN 55317-0326 • 800-599-READ • www.childsworld.com

Acknowledgments
The Child's World®: Mary Berendes, Publishing Director

Editorial Directions, Inc.: E. Russell Primm, Editorial Director; Pam Rosenberg, Line Editor; Katie Marsico, Assistant Editor; Matthew Messbarger, Editorial Assistant; Susan Hindman, Copy Editor; Susan Ashley, Proofreader; Julie Zaveloff, Chris Simms, and Peter Garnham, Fact Checkers; Tim Griffin/IndexServ, Indexer; Dawn Friedman, Photo Researcher; Linda S. Koutris, Photo Selector

The Design Lab: Kathleen Petelinsek, Art Direction; Kari Thornborough, Page Production

Photos
Cover/frontispiece: J. Stewart Wedding Party, Nekoma, ND, 1903.

Cover photographs ©: North Dakota Institute for Regional Studies, North Dakota State University/Fred Hulstrand Collection; Joseph Sohm, ChromoSohm Inc.

Interior photographs ©: AP/Wide World: 25; Bettmann/Corbis: 7, 9, 12, 16, 19, 20; Corbis: 6 (Ed Bohon), 17, 24 (Lee Snider; Lee Snider), 28 (Chuck Savage); Getty Images/Hulton Archive: 8, 10, 18, 22, 27; Historical Picture Archive/Corbis: 11, 13; North Wind Picture Archives: 14, 15.

Library of Congress Cataloging-in-Publication Data
Franchino, Vicky.
  British Americans / by Vicky Franchino.
    p. cm.— (Our cultural heritage)
  Includes index.
  Contents: English citizens in a new land—Breaking ties with England—From colonists to immigrants—The English influence.
  ISBN 1-59296-179-7 (Library Bound : alk. paper)
  1. British Americans—Juvenile literature. [1. British Americans.] I. Title. II. Series.
  E184.B7F73 2004
  973'.0413—dc22
                                    2003018093d

16   20   28

Contents

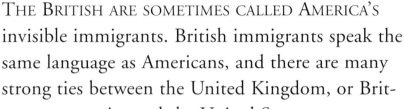

Chapter ONE

British Citizens in a New Land

Looking at this busy street in New York City, it is impossible to distinguish British Americans from other people in the crowd.

THE BRITISH ARE SOMETIMES CALLED AMERICA'S invisible immigrants. British immigrants speak the same language as Americans, and there are many strong ties between the United Kingdom, or Britain, and the United States.

The first 13 states were once colonies of Britain. Until the 1800s, most of the Europeans who lived in the United States were British. More than 5 million British immigrants have come to the United States. In the 2000 **census,** there were more than 31 million British Americans. They are the third-largest **ethnic** group in America.

Britain sent its first explorers to North America in 1497, just a few years after Christopher Columbus. That year, King Henry VII sent John

John Cabot (kneeling) explains his voyage to King Henry VII. Although Cabot ultimately landed in North America, it was initially hoped that the explorer would discover a shorter sea route to Asia.

Cabot (an Italian whose name was really Giovanni Caboto) to the Americas. When King Henry's granddaughter, Queen Elizabeth I, was in power (1558–1603), Britain set up its first colonies.

Colonies were useful to Britain for many reasons. They gave Britain a source of raw materials—such as wood and cotton—to use in making things. They offered people a chance for a better life. This was especially important when there weren't enough jobs in Britain. In the colonies, people could have religious freedom. Throughout Europe, people were often treated badly if their religion wasn't accepted by most people.

The first permanent colony was Jamestown, Virginia. A group of men called the London Com-

Interesting Fact

John Cabot set sail in 1496 but never made it across the Atlantic Ocean. He had to turn back because he did not have enough food on board his ship and the weather was very bad. He had better luck on his 1497 voyage.

pany set up this colony in 1607. The company paid for three ships and supplies, and 104 men traveled to America in search of riches and gold.

What they found instead were hardship, sickness, and death. Jamestown was swampy and full of mosquitoes. The water was not good, and many of the men became sick. To make matters worse, the colonists were not successful at growing food. There was also a terrible drought. By 1608, only 38 of the men were still alive.

More colonists came to Jamestown over the next few years. The colony was still not successful. Finally, in 1612, a surprising crop saved them— tobacco. The colonists discovered that the land in Virginia was very good for growing tobacco. This was a popular product in Europe.

Settlers in Jamestown load tobacco onto ships bound for England. By 1639, the colonists at Jamestown had exported 750 tons of tobacco.

The Pilgrims' voyage on the Mayflower *lasted 66 days and wasn't comfortable. People became seasick and didn't have much privacy on the crowded ship.*

Another important early colony was Plymouth, Massachusetts. This colony was founded in 1620. About half of the Plymouth colonists were Pilgrims. They belonged to a religious group called Separatists. They did not want to follow the Church of England—the official religion in Britain. In Britain, they suffered because of their beliefs. The Pilgrims hoped they would be able to practice their religion freely in the Americas.

A group of Pilgrims set sail on a ship called the *Mayflower.* They landed at Plymouth in November and had a hard first winter. There was very little food, and many of the colonists became sick. By spring, more than half the colonists had died.

Interesting Fact

▸ Pilgrim children and their parents did not take baths very often— probably only a few times each year! Like many people of their time, they believed that it was unhealthy to take too many baths. Today, we know that keeping clean is a good way to get rid of the germs that can make us sick.

▶ Britain discovered that the colonies were a good place to send criminals. Between 1607 and 1775, more than 50,000 British criminals were sent to the colonies because there was no room for them in the British prisons. In the colonies, criminals were forced to work for a certain amount of time, and then they were set free. Some of the criminals returned to Britain, but many stayed in America where they had the chance for a new life.

The Pilgrims found members of the Wampanoag tribe to be especially friendly and helpful. The two groups celebrated a thanksgiving feast that lasted three days and included approximately 90 Native Americans.

Luckily, the Pilgrims were helped by some friendly Native Americans. One, named Squanto, knew how to speak English. Squanto showed the Pilgrims how to plant corn. He taught them how to fertilize the soil and how to use plants to treat illness. To celebrate a good harvest, the Pilgrims shared a meal with their Native American neighbors. This first celebration is remembered each year on the holiday we call Thanksgiving.

As the years passed, Great Britain established more colonies in North America. By the mid-1700s, there were 13 in all.

MOST OF THE PEOPLE WHO LIVED IN THE COLONIES WERE FARMERS. THEY GREW crops and raised animals for their own families to use. Some colonists also sold farm products to Britain. Tobacco was one of the most important **export** crops because it was very popular in Britain. The climate and soil in Virginia and Maryland were perfect for growing tobacco.

The work of planting, caring for, and harvesting tobacco is hard. Many people are needed to do it. At first, colonial farmers used indentured servants. These were people who agreed to work for a farmer for a certain number of years. The farmer would pay for the indentured servant to travel on a ship from Britain. He would also give the servant food, a place to live, and some money. Although being an indentured servant was not an easy life, it was one way to get to America. Thousands of British people first came to the colonies as indentured servants.

As the tobacco farms grew, farmers started to use a new group of workers—slaves. Slaves were African or Caribbean men and women who had been brought to the British colonies in America. They were forced to work and did not receive any pay. The slaves were bought and sold like animals. Slave labor was cheaper than that of indentured servants, and slaves had to work for their owners for life.

Breaking Ties with Britain

▶ The area known as Virginia in early colonial times is not the same as today's state of Virginia. The original Virginia included most of the eastern coast of the United States. The name was in honor of Queen Elizabeth I. She was called the Virgin Queen.

OVER TIME, THE COLONIES GREW AND BECAME VERY successful. They were able to support themselves— and they also helped to support Britain. The colonies sent raw materials (lumber, cotton, tobacco, and furs) and finished goods (ships, tools, and household items) to Britain.

Barrels wait to be loaded onto ships in the Georgia Colony. Colonists in Georgia shipped rice, clay, pottery, cotton, indigo, tobacco, fruit, and pork across the Atlantic Ocean to Great Britian.

As the colonists grew more successful, they became frustrated with Britain. They believed they were treated unfairly by the government. As British citizens they expected to have certain rights. But as British colonists they had very little control over the way they were governed. The colonies were governed by the British **Parliament,** but there were no colonists in the Parliament. The colonists had no say in the government. They had to obey laws they hadn't helped to make. They had to pay taxes to the British government.

Even though they had no say in the British government, most colonists were proud to belong

The British House of Commons meets during the 1700s. The House of Commons is one branch of the British Parliament—the other branch is the House of Lords.

13

to the British Empire. They were loyal to the king and Parliament. But even though they remained loyal to Great Britain, some people did not have strong ties to Britain. Many colonial families had lived in America for four or five generations. Some had never even been to Britain!

Then, from 1756 to 1763, the Seven Years' War—also known as the French and Indian War— was fought between Britain and France for control of North America. This war changed how many colonists felt about Britain. Although Britain won, the war was very expensive and the colonies were expected to help pay for it. Britain passed laws such as the Sugar Act and the Stamp Act to raise money. These acts meant the colonists

British troops march to Fort Duquesne in Pennsylvania during the French and Indian War. Native Americans sided with the French during this conflict. The two groups already shared a successful trading relationship, and Native Americans feared the British would take over more of their land.

had to pay extra money for sugar, cloth, coffee, certain types of wine, and all paper documents.

Some of the colonists fought back against these laws. They refused to pay taxes. They ignored British rules. Sometimes they were put in jail. These colonists, who also wanted to form a separate country, were called Rebels or Patriots. Those who wanted the colonies to remain British and were **loyal** to the British government were called

The Declaration of Independence was signed in Philadelphia, Pennsylvania, by 56 colonial leaders. Future president Thomas Jefferson (placing papers on desk) was the author.

Loyalists or Tories. These feelings divided friends and sometimes even families.

In April 1775, the American Revolution broke out between Britain and the colonies. On July 4, 1776, colonial political leaders signed the Declaration of Independence. This said that the colonies were now a separate country called the United States of America. The war finally ended in 1781, and a treaty was signed in 1783.

The Patriots had won. The people were no longer British colonists. They were now Americans.

THOMAS EDISON (BELOW) WAS A FAMOUS INVENTOR AND SCIENTIST WHO knew it could take years of hard work to turn a good idea into a workable item. Edison once said, "Genius is 1 percent inspiration and 99 percent perspiration." Edison's ancestors were British Loyalists who moved to Canada during the American Revolution. They returned to the United States in the 1830s. As a child, Edison was often sick, and some of his teachers thought that he wasn't very smart! His mother always believed in him, and that helped Edison to have faith in himself.

Edison was an inventor who proved just how useful electricity could be. Some of his work improved the inventions of other people—like the telegraph and the telephone. Other inventions were things that he designed himself. His most important inventions were the electric lightbulb, the phonograph, and an early movie projector known as a kinetoscope. All together, Edison held patents on 1,093 inventions.

Chapter THREE

From Colonists to Immigrants

THERE WAS VERY LITTLE IMMIGRATION FROM BRITAIN to the United States right after the American Revolution. Loyal British citizens did not feel comfortable moving to their former colony. Many Tories who had lived in America for years decided to move back to Britain after the war.

The United States fought a second war with Britain—the War of 1812 (1812–1815). Britain tried

The USS Constitution *(right) sinks a British ship off the coast of Newfoundland during the War of 1812. Even though the famous American ship was made of wood, a sailor observed that some of the British cannonballs appeared to bounce off its sides. Today, many people still refer to the USS* Constitution *as "Old Ironsides."*

18

During England's Industrial Revolution, the poor faced terrible living and working conditions. Those people lucky enough to have jobs worked long hours for little money. Many were forced to live in crowded and dirty areas called slums where they often didn't even have access to fresh water.

to take control of the cities of Baltimore, Maryland; New Orleans, Louisiana; and Washington, D.C. The United States tried to take control of British territory in Canada. There was no clear winner of this war. Some historians say that the war proved the United States was truly independent from Britain.

After this war, the British began immigrating to the United States again. Britain's **Industrial Revolution** had begun in the 1700s. Since that time, there had been many changes in how products were made and how land was farmed. It became more common for machines to do many of the jobs that people had done in the past. As a result, many people lost their jobs. Others were forced to work in terrible conditions in crowded, dirty factories.

Interesting Fact

▶ A lawyer named Francis Scott Key wrote a poem called "The Star-Spangled Banner" after watching the British attack on Fort McHenry in 1814 (during the War of 1812). The poem was later set to music and became the U.S. national anthem.

European immigrants arrive in New York City, which came to be known as the "Golden Door" because of the large number of immigrants who entered the country there.

British workers hoped their skills would still be valued in the United States. Between 1815 and 1860, more than a half million British immigrants traveled to the United States in search of a better life for themselves and their families.

At that time, the trip to America was dangerous and hard. It could take up to two months to travel across the ocean. The ships that most British immigrants traveled on were really not meant to carry people. They carried lumber, cotton, and tobacco from the United States to Britain. On the return voyage, they carried people who wished to immigrate to the United States. Passengers slept on rough bunk beds and ate terrible food. Many people became ill—and some died—during the journey.

British immigrants usually settled in cities in the Northeast. They could not find jobs in the South, where most of the work was done by slaves. Sometimes all of the employees from a factory would move to the United States together. This was common in the **textile** industry. A factory owner might decide he could be more successful in America. If he didn't want to train new employees, the owner would move everyone to the United States together. Although the pay was better than in Britain, hours were still very long and the work was hard. Most people worked at least 11 hours a day, six days a week.

Few people immigrated to the United States during the Civil War (1861–1865), but after the war millions of British citizens came to America. While many still moved to cities in the Northeast, a growing number decided to go west. Although there were many risks and life could be very lonely, the wide-open prairies meant freedom and opportunity.

For many years, life in the United States felt very "British." This changed in the late 1800s. Immigrants poured into the country from Italy, Ireland, Poland, and Germany. Most did not speak English and did not have an education. They were desperate for work. There was much more competition for jobs that did not require any training.

British Americans often looked down on these new immigrants and thought they didn't belong. Even though the British were immigrants themselves, they were often unkind to immigrants who had a harder time fitting in. Many new immigrants lived in small communities with other people from their home country. They wanted to be near people who spoke their language and understood their customs. This was not true for the British. There was no reason for them to depend on one another. They spoke the language of America. They fit in at work, school, and church.

British immigrants continued to arrive in the United States during the 1900s, but there were not as many as in the past. Young men were more likely to immigrate than women or families. But many young British men died during World War I (1914–1918) and World War II (1939–1945). There was one special group of immigrants after World War II—war brides! Millions of U.S. soldiers were in Britain during the war, and more than 100,000 of them brought home British wives.

In the 1950s, laws changed and it became harder to immigrate to the United States. Now immigrants usually need to have a special skill to come to America. Immigrants who come from Britain today are usually well educated. Many are doctors, engineers, or computer programmers.

People of British descent live in every part of the United States. The largest numbers live in the southeast part of the country, as well as in California, Texas, Florida, New York, and Ohio.

U.S. soldiers in London sitting arm-in-arm with female members of that city's Auxiliary Fire Service. During World War II, these women helped extinguish fires that were caused when enemy planes dropped bombs in the area.

ALTHOUGH THE UNITED STATES AND BRITAIN SHARE A LANGUAGE, there are many words that are different. Here are just a few:

American	British
apartment	flat
argument	row
baby carriage	pram (short for perambulator)
Band-Aid	plaster
bathroom	loo or WC
can	tin
cookie	biscuit
diaper	nappy
elevator	lift
expressway	motorway
flashlight	torch
fries	chips
gas	petrol
guy	bloke, chap
hood (car)	bonnet
license plate	number plate
line	queue
mail	post
napkin	serviette
pacifier	dummy
parking lot	car park
potato chips	crisps
rent	hire
soccer	football
sweater	jumper
trash can	bin
truck	lorry
trunk (car)	boot
windshield (car)	windscreen

Chapter FOUR

The British Influence

THE BRITISH ARE SO MUCH A PART OF AMERICA THAT it's easy to forget the many ways they helped to shape the country. Many of the ideas and traditions that might be considered American are actually British!

Language is one of the most important things that Britain and the United States share. Although

Saint James Episcopal Church was built in South Carolina in 1768. More than 1 million Americans are members of the Episcopal faith, which is one of several Protestant religions practiced in the United States.

24

America is home to many languages, English has been the common language since colonial times.

British religions have helped to shape this country. Many of the early settlers were members of various Protestant religions. Today, roughly half of the adults in the United States belong to some type of Protestant religion. In many northeastern states, there is a long **tradition** of simple living and **frugality**—things that were valued by the early Puritans who settled there.

The British also helped to shape the U.S. educational system. Many of the most well-known universities and colleges in America were founded during colonial times. Harvard University, the oldest university in the United States, opened in 1636. Princeton University opened in 1746, and Yale University in 1701.

Nassau Hall at Princeton University was used as a hospital for both British and American troops during the Revolutionary War. In addition, the Continental Congress met there from July through November in 1783.

▶ According to some historians, the cotton gin was responsible for keeping slavery alive in the southern United States. Even though the cotton gin made removing the seeds from cotton much easier, it also increased the need for slave labor. Cotton became a very profitable crop and farmers wanted to grow as much of it as they could. They needed more slaves to plant and harvest the cotton and more land to grow it on. In 1790, only two years before Eli Whitney invented his cotton gin, there were six slave states in the United States. In 1860 there were 15 slave states in the United States.

The founding leaders of the United States looked to Britain for ideas when setting up their new government. The U.S. Bill of Rights limits the power of the government. It also gives citizens certain rights, such as freedom of speech. It was based on the British Bill of Rights, which was written in 1689.

Thomas Jefferson wrote the Declaration of Independence after reading the Englishman John Locke's writings. Locke was a **philosopher** who believed that all human beings were born equal and had the freedom to pursue "life, health, liberty, and possessions." He also believed that people had the right to free speech and thought. These ideas were important parts of Jefferson's Declaration of Independence.

Most of the early leaders of the United States had ties to Britain. Throughout the history of America, many political leaders have been of British heritage. More than half of America's presidents have British **ancestors.**

Many different industries in America got their start with the help of British knowledge, workers, and investors. The textile industry had many links to Britain. The cotton industry was dominated by Britain until the cotton gin completely changed the American cotton industry in the late 1700s. This machine removed the seeds from cotton—a job that took a lot of time when it was done by hand.

Many other industries came to the United States from Britain. Carpet makers and steel workers settled in Pennsylvania. Lace makers moved to Brooklyn, New York. Almost the entire British silk industry moved to the United States after the Civil War. Ironworkers came to New York, and miners went to Illinois. Printers also arrived in Illinois as well as Massachusetts. Many of these industries can still be found in these areas today.

People might be surprised to know that the "all-American" sport of baseball is actually a version of a British children's game called rounders. Rounders can be traced back to the 1500s. A version of the game is still played today in Britain.

American literature and music have many ties to Britain. Some of America's most famous authors and poets are of British descent. Edgar Allan Poe, William Faulkner, Robert Frost, and Emily Dickinson are just a few. Many American folk songs have their roots in traditional British folk songs.

Emily Dickinson left behind nearly 2,000 poems when she died in 1886. She is still considered one of America's greatest poets.

Some of the most popular American holiday traditions also came from Britain. At Christmastime, people often go door-to-door singing Christmas carols. This tradition started in Britain in the Middle Ages (350–1450).

British immigrants have been coming to North America for more than 500 years. They played a leading role in the creation of the United States. Perhaps more than any other group, they have influenced the history and culture of America. While the British may be "invisible immigrants," their contributions have visibly shaped the United States of today.

Caroling began when British musicians wandered from town to town to perform at castles or the homes of the rich. Although they hoped to receive food or money for their performances, most carolers today carry on the tradition for their own enjoyment and the pleasure they bring to the people they visit.

1497   King Henry VII sends John Cabot to explore the Americas.

1584   Queen Elizabeth I gives explorer Walter Raleigh permission to establish colonies in North America.

1587   Virginia Dare is the first British colonist born in America.

1606   King James I establishes the Virginia Company of London in the hopes of finding gold in America.

1607   The British colony at Jamestown is founded.

1620   The Pilgrims leave Britain seeking religious freedom and found a colony at Plymouth, Massachusetts.

1756–1763   The British fight the French in North America in what becomes known as the French and Indian War.

1765   The British tax the colonists with the Stamp Act, which causes widespread protests and rioting.

1770   Five American colonists are killed by British soldiers in a fight that becomes known as the Boston Massacre.

1773   Colonists stage the Boston Tea Party in Boston Harbor to protest the British tax on tea.

1775   The American Revolution begins.

1776   Colonial leaders sign the Declaration of Independence and assert their freedom from British rule.

1781   The American Revolution ends.

1812–1815   The United States and Britain fight the War of 1812.

1815–1860   More than a half million British citizens emigrate to the United States in search of a better life.

1914–1918   World War I is fought.

1939–1945   World War II is fought; U.S. soldiers bring home more than 100,000 British war brides.

ancestors (AN-sess-turz)
Members of your family who lived a long time ago are your ancestors. Many U.S. presidents had British ancestors.

census (SEN-suhss)
A census is an official count of the number of people in a country or area. The 2000 census showed that the British are the third-largest group in the United States.

ethnic (ETH-nik)
This term describes a group of people who have the same language, culture, or other traits. The British are the third-largest ethnic group in the United States.

export (EK-sport)
An export is a product sold to another country. Tobacco was one of the colonies' most important exports.

frugality (froo-GAHL-uh-tee)
Frugality is the quality of managing money carefully. Puritan settlers were known for their frugality.

Industrial Revolution (in-DUHSS-tree-uhl rev-uh-LOO-shuhn)
The Industrial Revolution was a period that began in Britain in the 1700s; it was a time when things that were once made by hand or at home were made by machines and in factories. Many British citizens moved to the United States during the Industrial Revolution because they thought their talents would still be valuable there.

loyal (LOI-uhl)
To be loyal means to be faithful in your support of your country, family, or friends. Tories were colonists who were loyal to the British government.

Parliament (PAR-luh-muhnt)
Parliament is the part of government in Britain that is similar to Congress in the United States. The early colonists were frustrated because they did not have a voice in Parliament.

philosopher (fuh-LOSS-uh-fur)
A philosopher is a person who studies ideas that are basic to human life, such as truth, beauty, or what it means to be real. Thomas Jefferson was inspired by an English philosopher.

textile (TEK-stile)
A textile is a fabric. The British textile industry often moved entire factories of workers to the United States.

tradition (truh-DISH-uhn)
Tradition is the practice of handing down customs or beliefs from one generation to another. Some common United States traditions actually began in Britain.

For Further INFORMATION

Web Sites

Visit our homepage for lots of links about British Americans:
http://www.childsworld.com/links.html

Note to Parents, Teachers, and Librarians:
We routinely verify our Web links to make sure they're safe,
active sites—so encourage your readers to check them out!

Books

Herbert, Janis. *The American Revolution for Kids: A History with 21 Activities.*
Chicago: Chicago Review Press, 2002.

Moscinski, Sharon. *Tracing Our English Roots.* Santa Fe, N.M.: John Muir
Publications, 1995.

Sakurai, Gail. *The Jamestown Colony.* Danbury, Conn.: Children's Press, 1997.

Places to Visit or Contact

APVA Jamestown Rediscovery
To learn more about the British colony at Jamestown
1367 Colonial Parkway
Jamestown, VA 23081
757/229-0412

Edison National Historic Site
For a tour of Edison's research lab and estate
Main Street and Lakeside Avenue
West Orange, NJ 07052
973/736-0550, ext. 42

Index

About the Author

VICKY FRANCHINO HAS ALWAYS LOVED TO LEARN ABOUT THE PAST. SHE HAS fond memories of Laura Ingalls Wilder's "Little House" books—especially *The Long Winter*—and still has a picture of the papier-mâché castle she made in the 6th grade. She enjoyed the chance to learn more about the immigrants who have helped create the United States we know today. Vicky lives with her husband and their three daughters in Wisconsin.